FRANK LLOYD WRIGHT: DOMESTIC ARCHITECTURE AND OBJECTS

⊏━━━━━━━⊐ INTRODUCTION BY PATRICK J. MEEHAN, AIA ⊏━━━━━⊐

PRESERVATION PRESS
John Wiley & Sons, Inc.
New York Chichester Brisbane Toronto Singapore

Printed in South Korea by Sung In
5   4   3   2

ISBN 0-471-14501-7

Cover: Pope-Leighey House (1940), Mount Vernon, Virginia. (©1991 Ping Amranand)
Designed by Garruba Dennis Design, Washington, D.C.
Composed in Futura Book

Introduction

Frank Lloyd Wright (1867–1959) was one of the most prolific of American architects. During his long career of more than 70 years, he designed more than 1,100 projects. He once claimed on national television late in his career that ". . . it's quite easy for me to shake them out of my sleeve." His projects ranged from vases to buildings. From Wright's numerous commissions, many of which resulted only in drawings, slightly more than 500 structures were actually built, and of those, about one-fourth were residential buildings. Wright showed a special love for the construction of homes, perhaps dating back to his early days with the architectural firm Sullivan and Adler in Chicago, when, on the sly, he independently designed houses for clients in and around Oak Park, Illinois. That transgression led to his departure from the firm, at which point Wright set up his own firm, first in the Schiller Building in Chicago and then in Oak Park, in a studio attached to his own home. The collection of designs presented here spans Wright's residential work from 1889 to 1950 and includes his home and studio.

Sadly, more than 80 of Wright's structures have been demolished. But collectible remnants, such as the table and chairs from the now- gone Joseph W. Husser House, are also presented here. Wright's buildings were such great works of art that, even when dismantled by the wrecker's ball or bulldozer, the pieces remaining are distinctive works of art themselves–as if capturing a fleeting loose note or two from a great symphony.

This collection also shows the full breadth of the application of Wright's principles of "organic architecture." Wright defined organic architecture this way: "Where the whole is [to] the part as the part is to the whole and where the nature of the materials, the nature of purpose, the nature of the entire performance becomes a necessity." His view is evident in the various scale of his designs and their innate artistic complexity no matter what the scale, as well as the repetition of shapes and themes. Note particularly the detail of the side chair initially designed for the Barnsdall House and copied many years later by former Wright clients, the Lovnesses, and compare this detail to the Barnsdall House living room. Or compare the ornate art glass windows of the Dana-Thomas House to the view of its gallery room.

Another common thread here is the ease with which the public may view these extraordinary places. Most are under some form of public ownership or on display in museums or collections. Thus, Wright's great residential works have transcended singular private ownership status. Many of these sites were donated to the public because their owners felt strongly that no one is entitled to "own" such great works of art. They belong to all, for all to enjoy. They are timeless and belong to the ages.

Patrick J. Meehan, AIA

Master Bedroom.
Frank Lloyd Wright Home and Studio, 1889, Oak Park, Illinois

A vaulted ceiling expands into what Wright considered the useless space of the attic, giving a spacious feeling to this small room. The mural, along with a companion on the south wall, was painted by Orlando Giannini in 1895. During restoration of the home and studio in 1979, ten coats of paint were removed from the murals, which afterward were carefully restored. The home and studio is a property of the National Trust for Historic Preservation.

Photo by Jon Miller, Hedrich-Blessing.
From *Frank Lloyd Wright: Domestic Architecture and Objects,*
published by The Preservation Press, National Trust for Historic Preservation ©1991.

Stork Panels.
Frank Lloyd Wright Home and Studio, 1889, Oak Park, Illinois

These panels, designed by Wright and executed for him by sculptor Richard W. Bock, decorate the columns gracing the entrance to Wright's studio, added in 1898. The panel designs include the tree of life, the book of knowledge, a scroll of architectural plans, and sentry storks, possibly symbols of wisdom or fertility. The home and studio is a property of the National Trust for Historic Preservation.

Photo by Robert Llewellyn.
From *Frank Lloyd Wright: Domestic Architecture and Objects,*
published by The Preservation Press, National Trust for Historic Preservation ©1991.

Library.
Meyer May House, 1908, Grand Rapids, Michigan

Frank Lloyd Wright positioned the T-shaped house to provide maximum southern exposure for skylights and windows. Here the window design is echoed in the table runner embroidery and carpet pattern. Purchased by Steelcase, Inc., in 1985, the house has been restored.

Photo by Hedrich-Blessing.
From *Frank Lloyd Wright: Domestic Architecture and Objects,*
published by The Preservation Press, National Trust for Historic Preservation ©1991.

Dining Table and Side Chairs.
Joseph W. Husser House, 1899, Chicago, Illinois

Sole survivor of the demolished Husser House, this set of oak furniture represents the severe rectilinear forms Frank Lloyd Wright experimented with in his early furniture designs. The seats are covered in leather.

Photo courtesy of the Domino's Pizza Collection.
From *Frank Lloyd Wright: Domestic Architecture and Objects,*
published by The Preservation Press, National Trust for Historic Preservation ©1991.

Art Glass Window.
Dana-Thomas House, 1902, Springfield, Illinois

Frank Lloyd Wright chose the sumac as the dominating plant theme in his designs for the Dana-Thomas House, as evidenced in this window in the reception hall. Sconces bracket the window. Some 450 pieces of art glass and more than 100 pieces of oak furniture were included in the original commission from Springfield socialite Susan Lawrence Dana.

Photo by Bill Crofton. Courtesy of the Dana-Thomas House Foundation.
From *Frank Lloyd Wright: Domestic Architecture and Objects,*
published by The Preservation Press, National Trust for Historic Preservation ©1991.

Dana-Thomas House, 1902, Springfield, Illinois

No expense was spared when Frank Lloyd Wright designed this house for Springfield socialite Susan Lawrence Dana. The house, one of the best examples of Wright's Prairie architecture, incorporates a gallery and studio not seen in this view of the south facade. It is now administered by the Illinois Historic Preservation Agency.

Gallery.
Dana-Thomas House, 1902, Springfield, Illinois

Reopened in 1990 after a three-year, $5 million restoration, the house contains the largest collection of original Frank Lloyd Wright–designed furniture and art glass of any of the architect's structures. The gallery, often used for entertaining, is an expansive barrel-vaulted space. One of three balconies located throughout the house provides an area for musicians to entertain guests.

©1991 Judith Bromley. Courtesy of the Dana-Thomas House Foundation.
From *Frank Lloyd Wright: Domestic Architecture and Objects,*
published by The Preservation Press, National Trust for Historic Preservation ©1991.

Double-Pedestal Table Lamp.
Dana-Thomas House, 1902, Springfield, Illinois

This art glass and bronze lamp was one of several designed for the house. This particular lamp sits on a studio table in the living room of the house designed for Springfield socialite Susan Lawrence Dana by Frank Lloyd Wright.

Reclining Armchair.
Arthur Heurtley House, 1902, Oak Park, Illinois

Designed to complement the living room of the Heurtley House, now divided into two apartments, this birch and elm armchair designed by Frank Lloyd Wright expresses a solidity and angularity reflected in the house's square plan and projecting window bays.

Courtesy of the Domino's Pizza Collection.
From *Frank Lloyd Wright: Domestic Architecture and Objects,*
published by The Preservation Press, National Trust for Historic Preservation ©1991.

Fabric (Design No. 104)

In 1955 Frank Lloyd Wright embarked on a series, called "The Taliesin Line," of fabric and wallpaper designs for F. Schumacher & Company, New York City. This particular design, made of silk and Fortisan casement, is based on the floor plans of residences Wright designed for his sons Robert Llewellyn Wright and David Wright.

Edgar J. Kaufmann, Sr., Residence
(Fallingwater), 1935, Mill Run, Pennsylvania

The most famous of Frank Lloyd Wright's buildings, Fallingwater was built as a vacation home for Pittsburgh department store magnate Edgar J. Kaufmann, Sr. The house perches over a waterfall and seems to grow out of the rocks to which it is anchored. Made of reinforced concrete and sandstone quarried on site, Fallingwater comes closest of any of Wright's houses to exemplifying the unity of man and nature which the architect spoke of so often.

Photo by Robert Llewellyn.
From *Frank Lloyd Wright: Domestic Architecture and Objects,*
published by The Preservation Press, National Trust for Historic Preservation ©1991.

Pope-Leighey House, 1940, Mount Vernon, Virginia

Built of cypress, brick, and glass, the house exemplifies Frank Lloyd Wright's concept of the Usonian home: a basementless single-story home of modular design, including a carport and heated floor slab. Originally constructed for newspaper journalist Loren Pope at Falls Church, Virginia, the house was moved in 1964 to Woodlawn Plantation to escape demolition. It is a property of the National Trust for Historic Preservation.

Aline Barnsdall House
(Hollyhock House), 1919–21, Los Angeles, California

One of 45 buildings commissioned by Aline Barnsdall, oil heiress and theater producer, this residence is reminiscent of a Mayan temple. Its decorative motif and name are derived from Barnsdall's favorite flower. Of the three structures Frank Lloyd Wright built for Barnsdall's planned arts community, only two survive. Others were designed but never executed. The house is owned by the city of Los Angeles.

Photo by Kirk McDonald.
From *Frank Lloyd Wright: Domestic Architecture and Objects,*
published by The Preservation Press, National Trust for Historic Preservation ©1991.

Living Room.
Aline Barnsdall House(Hollyhock House), 1919–21, Los Angeles, California

Frank Lloyd Wright designed the living room around two oak sofas that focused on the fireplace and reflecting pool. Attached writing tables with light towers provided for a diverse use of space. The lost furniture was reconstructed and installed in 1990 by the city of Los Angeles, which owns the property.

Lovness Side Chair.
Donald and Virginia Lovness Cottage, 1958–76, Stillwater, Minnesota

Originally designed in 1920 for the Hollyhock House, a set of these side chairs was commissioned by the Lovnesses for their cottage, built near the end of Frank Lloyd Wright's life. The oak chairs were created through a time-consuming layering process.

Charles Ennis Residence, 1923, Los Angeles, California

The last of four textile-block houses Frank Lloyd Wright designed in the Los Angeles area, the Ennis house is the most monumental. The blocks were cast in molds and reinforced with steel rods. The finished patterned and plain blocks were then stacked together without visible mortar joints, providing an interesting play of light and pattern across the surface.

Photo by Tim Street-Porter.
From *Frank Lloyd Wright: Domestic Architecture and Objects,*
published by The Preservation Press, National Trust for Historic Preservation ©1991.

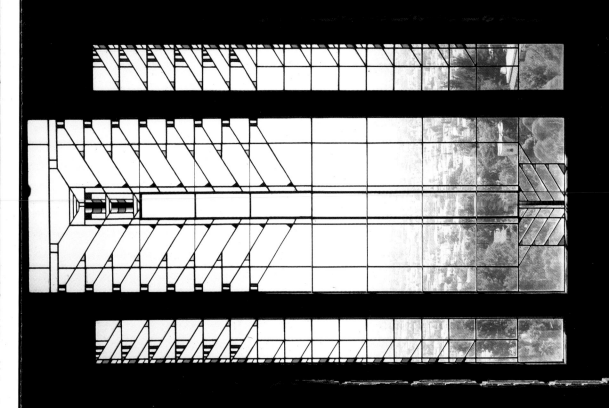

Art Glass Window.
Charles Ennis Residence, 1923, Los Angeles, California

The art glass windows for the Ennis Residence were the last Frank Lloyd Wright designed. Hereafter he favored clear plate glass for all of his structures. This window continues the play of light and shadow found on the exterior's textile-block surface

Photo by Tim Street-Porter.
From *Frank Lloyd Wright: Domestic Architecture and Objects,*
published by The Preservation Press, National Trust for Historic Preservation ©1991.

Living Room.
John Storer Residence, 1923, Hollywood, California

The second of Frank Lloyd Wright's four textile-block houses in the Los Angeles area, the Storer Residence featured this two-story-high living room on the second floor. The lowest story of the house was devoted to work spaces.

Photo by Tim Street-Porter.
From *Frank Lloyd Wright: Domestic Architecture and Objects,*
published by The Preservation Press, National Trust for Historic Preservation ©1991.

Isadore J. and Lucille Zimmerman House, 1950, Manchester, New Hampshire

Reflecting elements of Frank Lloyd Wright's Prairie and Usonian houses, the Zimmerman House has been restored by the Currier Gallery of Art and is now open to the public. The house, composed of concrete block and cypress, is sited diagonally on a one-acre lot. Its extensive band of windows on the south facade brings the outside almost directly into the house and overlooks gardens also designed by Wright.

Photo by Richard Cheek.
From *Frank Lloyd Wright: Domestic Architecture and Objects,*
published by The Preservation Press, National Trust for Historic Preservation ©1991.